SIMPLE FAT BURN

Three Steps to Becoming
Fit & Lean

Cover design by Kristen Lewter
Cover photos by Fox Gradin
Text design by Jennifer Wright

Second Edition
978-0-9905147-2-5

SIMPLE FAT BURN

Three Steps to Becoming Fit & Lean

Cathryn Marshall, MSW

Cathryn Marshall | Simple Fat Burn

2015

Dedication

I give infinite thanks to my loving parents and stepparents. My Mom, Susan, who always told me I was a leader, not a follower. My Dad, Jerry, who only missed 5 days of work due to funerals in 35 years of service. My stepfather, Bob, who has the best sense of humor, ever. And my Stepmother, Dolly, who asked "So when are you going to write your book?"

Acknowledgements

Thank you to my clients, without your hard work and commitment to transformation, none of this exists to help others. You've been my teachers and reason for being on the planet. I come from a long line of educators. My grandmother Emogene, Aunt Mabel and Mother were all educators. At times they seemed dismayed I was not going to become a schoolteacher. Clearly, I have become an educator of fitness and nutrition due to their influence. Often I think of and refer to the many teachers who educated me throughout grade school. Although I was no model student as a teenager, your education and wisdom truly had an impact. My college professors gave me incredible insight in helping others to the best of my ability. My Grandmother Eleanor Rucker taught me to be kind and tolerant. I am indebted to my business mentors and coaches. I am especially grateful to Andy Lowe and Renee Walkup. I often think everyone should be so lucky to have such awesome advice.

Thank you to the people who gave me a chance at the many jobs and internships I worked at. A. Sam and Son's, McDonald's and The Vineyard were my first jobs that taught me tenacity and the value of hard work. John Krebs, you were my start in business and a great influence in my life. Tom Quinn, you were the best boss and first employer who told me we would "throw anyone out" upon my request.

I must acknowledge with great thanks the many personal trainers who taught me, trained me, and mentored me throughout my career. My first trainer, JD, wherever you are, you trained me right. For the very highest levels of personal training specializations, I give huge thanks to Robert Autry, Randy Nicholson and Kathy Mulherin.

Thank you, George Turmon, IFBB Pro Bodybuilder, my trainer, mentor, friend and unofficial therapist. I have been incredibly happy working with you all these years and have learned so much while having fun.

I give special thanks to Phil Kaplan, the master of personal training and my first fitness business mentor. Your education truly shaped my career and because of you, thousands of personal training clients have been transformed for the better. Your insight, passion for fitness, encouragement and friendship is truly a rare and priceless gift.

Thank you to my sweet close friends, who have always supported me, my work and my over loaded schedule. Much love to Deana,

Arlene, Cathy W., Cathy V., Anna, Eunice, Carol, Adela, Tonya, Kim, Christa, Alicia, Helen, Patrick, Linda, Greta and Kathy. I am honored to call you friends and family. Thank you Patti, you infuse FUN into everything. Thank you Joe Harrison, for training with me and entertaining me for 16 years. Many thanks to Jim and Freddie, your suggestions have made this book a reality.

A big "Thank You" to Jennifer Wright, for your inspiration, friendship, dedication to your own fitness, and expertise as a writer.

Thank you, Dr. Joyce Rennolds, "Motivator of one or a thousand". Your mentoring and education has been the best. You motivate me!

Thank you to my son, Cameron Scott Marshall. Your laughter makes my day.

Introduction

This book is written first and foremost to be exactly what I do: act as a catalyst for positive change. Its sole purpose is to offer a simple strategy with tools to attain a higher level of health and fitness. Simple Fat Burn is a compilation of 17 years of experience as a personal trainer and nutrition educator. This is combined with a diverse educational background that includes a Master's degree in Social Work. It is designed to produce massive results for re-configuration and lasting change.

In three simple steps you can transform, from the inside out, to burn fat immediately and maintain a lean body for life. The highest purpose Simple Fat Burn can fulfill is to bring joy, happiness and inner peace to those who engage in the concepts. It works for people of all ages. It is simple and the results are exponential.

Contents

PART I:
My Story

1. My Story:
How I Arrived Here

I have followed several paths in my life. As a child and teen, I spent a decade in ballet with many lead roles. I aspired to join a dance troupe and become a professional ballerina. Standing 4'11' with a curvy body type, I realized at 14 that I would never become a prima ballerina. For me, however, anything less than being the best would not be acceptable. My mother told me that I was a "leader, not a follower." Funny, now she doesn't even remember saying that.

Being driven for success at a young age, I shifted my educational path into art. I was a good enough artist to win scholarships and be chosen to design the cover of our graduation ceremony program. I was paid to create some signs and portraits in college. But I lacked patience and focus. I knew that the 10,000 paintings it would take for me to actually become an accomplished artist were not going to happen with my lack of discipline. After a fun year as an art student, I dropped out of college to find my passion. I moved from New York to Florida, took a job in a factory, and enrolled in a career-planning course.

I returned to college the next year and obtained my B.S. in Sociology. I went on to complete my Masters' degree in Social Work at SUNY Buffalo. At 26, I was working in Buffalo, NY, as a medical social worker for Millard Fillmore Hospital, seeing clients for counseling and case management. This was a great position for me until I found myself entirely burned out. My eating habits were out of control. I knew how to endlessly give to my clients and work long hours, but was clueless as to how to take care of myself. I took two years off and once again found myself looking to decide upon a new and fulfilling career.

THE TRANSFORMATION
I moved to Atlanta, married and had my son Cameron in '87. I forged ahead with a decision to start a new career as a personal trainer. I was struggling with weight gain. I ate excessive amounts of sugar, bread, pasta and processed foods. My diet was a mess. After Cameron was born, I had 34 pounds of fat to lose. Keep in mind that I am 4'11". With those 34 extra pounds, I felt like a stuffed sausage. When my baby was just two weeks old, I started running. This was in Atlanta (Hotlanta), with over 90 degree temperatures. I just needed to get the fat off.

I was overweight, deconditioned, exhausted and uncomfortable. When Cameron was two months old, I was in the gym with my first trainer, J.D. The workouts saved my sanity. I was going through an extremely rough home life, a career crisis and truly felt stress levels higher than I had ever imagined I could experience on a regular basis. During my training sessions with J.D., I felt grounded and in control. I knew I was doing something positive for myself that would one day help me help others.

I did exactly what my trainer told me to do. Specifically, I ate exactly what my trainer told me to eat. In 90 days, I had lost the 34 pounds. J.D., I don't know where you are today, but I am indebted to you for your training, friendship, counseling, mentoring and my career.

Thankfully, I got lean, fit, educated and have gone on to help thousands of others re-configure their lives from fat to fit and unhealthy to healthy. I found that in order to transform requires one to look at the not only the physical aspect, but also the mental and emotional dimensions. Transforming both the mind and body has a direct correlation to a better mental state of being. I closed the gap from my social work career to bridge the mental and physical aspects of well-being. The scenarios that eluded me as a student and as a social worker seemed to finally come together and make sense.

2. The A-B-Cs For Living A Lean Fit Life

How do we get and stay lean and fit for the rest of our lives?

How do we have endless energy and optimal health?

How do we change the way we think and act and in turn change the way we feel?

How do we create a new and improved version of our former selves?

The formula is simple and it can lead us to a new state of mental, physical, emotional and social well-being. We can create a new and improved version of our former selves. A change in overall consistent behavior is necessary to evoke a transformed body. Behavior modification is one of the key concepts in becoming permanently healthier and leaner with lots more energy. The best part of this is that this type of change is simple.

SIMPLE FAT BURN

There are three simple steps to being lean and fit:

A – Low glycemic meals – balanced nutrition

B – Move your body - exercise

C – Consciousness – awareness

Insulin (also known as blood sugar) is a hormone that tells your body when to store fat. When insulin spikes, it triggers fat to be stored in the cells. When you are able to keep your blood sugar consistent, your body can burn fat with ease.

Simple Fat Burn Concept: Changing your actions will change your body, your mind and your spirit.

As behavior changes and we consistently eat low glycemic meals, blood sugar levels cease to spike and fat is not stored in the cells.

JUDY'S STORY
I met Judy at The Cecil B. Day Sports and Fitness Center where I spent 11 years managing the personal training department and working as a personal trainer. Judy was in her late 60's, obese and had suffered a heart attack. She spent years caring for loved ones who passed from cancer and was now caring for her disabled husband who needed full-time nursing care. After her cardiac rehab program, she followed the fitness and

nutrition instructions she was given. She lost 15 pounds. Judy was by far one of the most dedicated, driven clients I have ever met. Within one year she transformed from an obese woman to a slim fit and vibrant woman. She lost over 50 pounds by exercising consistently, maintaining a food journal and keeping her focus on the outcome. Her attitude was exceptional. Her transformation was, and still is, amazing. She did strength training, yoga, cardiovascular exercise, took a variety of classes and ate balanced meals. She took every bit of my advice and expertise and put it to work on a daily basis.

3. The Strategy

YOU HAVE FREEDOM

I like to keep things simple. I have an inherent respect for minimalism. Less is more, and it really is easy and concise with the correct strategy. There are two simple rules for the Simple Fat Burn process.

RULE NUMBER 1:
There is nothing you have to do!

Yes, really. You don't have to lose weight, get lean and fit or even finish reading this book. You don't have to do any of it. I often tell people this to let them know they really do have options. It's called free will. YOU are in the driver's seat.

Simple Fat Burn Concept: You have to "opt in" and start to take action to get any kind of result.

The choice is yours to make.

If you've ever had to study for an exam or get a degree, "opting in" is critical to getting the task done. If you don't believe me on this rule, just look at some of your friends and family members. Think about their successes. People make a choice and take action to be successful. I always find this idea quite freeing. My close friend Arlene and I joke about this. If in doubt, refer to rule #1.

RULE NUMBER 2:
Everything you think and say is having an effect.

We all create our reality. Your body fat percentage is a result of what you think, say, feel and do. If you are familiar with quantum physics, it is where spirituality and science meet with proof that on some level you are creating your life.

Perhaps some of the things you are creating and attracting into your life are on a subconscious level. These subconscious thoughts can also be changed. If there are negative, unwanted, old programmed 'images' in your subconscious, no worries! Consciously determine what it is that you do want in your life – a change in your circumstance will soon follow. Once a better thought is introduced, a positive action will follow. I often listen to what clients are saying about their bodies and compare that to their results. I call it "listening between the words". Clients will tell me their story and exactly where change needs to happen for them.

Taking quantum physics further - even thinking about someone has an effect on both the one who holds the thoughts and the subject of the thoughts. What you think about your family, friends, co-workers and yourself is being created thought by thought. What you say and write also has an effect.

Simple Fat Burn Concept: We can create a clear outcome based on thoughts, feelings, words, and actions with an effective strategy.

That's it, just two simple rules for getting fit and lean.

1. There is nothing you have to do.
2. Everything you think and say is having an effect.

Both rules offer empowerment and a foundation for simply burning fat and being healthy for life. Take personal responsibility for your life, your health, and your fitness. Taking personal responsibility means putting all possibilities in your court. If you define your health and well-being by looking at yourself, you will take a huge step in creating a new reality. This is a great exercise you can do. Re-write your story, taking personalresponsibility.

MARINA'S STORY
Marina is the 16 year-old daughter of, Ava. One of my most successful personal training clients and friend, Sam Zimmerman, referred Ava to me. Ava hardly needed my services. Ava was

energetic, lean, works out, eats healthy and told me the last few pounds she needed to lose could "come off by osmosis". Yes, that's actually what she said, and I agreed with her.

Shortly after beginning to consult with Ava, she mentioned that she thought I could help her daughter, Marina. Ava left our consultation with no follow up appointment. I called to check on her, and she set an appointment for two weeks later to meet her daughter. On the day I was to meet Marina, it had been well over a month since I met Ava. It was a Saturday afternoon, and I was REALLY tired. Marina was the last of over 60 appointments for the week, she was 20 minutes late, and Ava was just then calling to say that she was on her way.

I was tired, exhausted in fact, on overload, and flat out done with appointments for the week. I was complaining – ranting actually - to George, my friend and confidant. I told him that I was leaving at 2pm no matter what. I told him I was burned out on clients for the week, and had little to no patience left. When Ava called, I asked her if she would like to re-schedule. She asked me to stay and just meet her daughter. I continued my rant to George who nodded, and agreed in support that it was just not acceptable to keep someone waiting this long on a Saturday afternoon.

Marina finally arrived and she sat in my office, looking miserable, obviously dragged in by her skinny Mom. I asked Marina to tell me about herself.

Her response:

"I'm fat and I've been on every diet since I was nine years old. All the girls in my school are skinny. Nothing works."

Marina was crying and suddenly I wanted to cry too. I asked myself, "How can this happen? Why can't we get a kid lean and healthy after being on every program out there?" Ava had clearly spent a lot of money, dragged her daughter to countless appointments, and signed up for several programs. They have done the work, and yet this 16 year old was 224lbs.

I listened to Marina's most recent bout with a medical weight loss program. She lost 35lbs and after getting off the program put all the weight right back on, again.

I explained the nutrition and workout plan to Marina and she said, "I think I can do this." I told Marina she didn't have to do any of this. It was totally up to her.

I was horrified thinking about my earlier thoughts and total lack of patience. I thought, "God help me be a better trainer with more patience". I went off to enjoy my weekend thinking about this. Six months later Marina had lost 30 pounds. We nicknamed her "VivaSkinnyMarina".

This experience taught me a lot about the choices we make. I love Marina and her sisters. Marina's mother, Ava, amazes me that she can work a full-time job, manage 4 children and look beautiful. Ava may be late for appointments, but that is really OK!

PART II:
Your Story

4. Your Motivation

Often clients ask how they can get motivated. I tell them to first, find out what excites and energizes you. The answer is to look at aspects of your life and listen to what your priorities are. The feelings and answers around this will surface.

I recently had a client mention that her husband promised her a trip to Hawaii for losing weight (her idea). Suddenly, she was totally motivated to get back on track after several months of eating off the plan and not exercising. Motivators will be directly related to your core values.

What are your true key motivators? There are both internal and external motivators. Internal motivators are based on values and feelings. External motivators are based on events. Neither is "good or bad". As a matter of course, in my teaching, we step away from the concepts of "good or bad" and "right or wrong". We only look at whether or not an action or belief will move you closer to your desired outcome.

Simple Fat Burn Concept: Acceptance and non-judgment within your strategy are far more powerful than being right or wrong.

Much of the philosophy that applies here depends on "how much and how often" as part of the process. Forging a better way with thoughts and actions serving the new picture is where **change truly happens.** What we are going for is an outcome that personally works for you. "I want to lose 25-30lbs", is not a clear outcome. "I lose 30lbs with ease by July 4th", is a clear outcome. No waffling. You can always shift gears and change your specific outcome at any given time.

INTERNAL MOTIVATORS

Knowing your own personal motivators off the top of your head is a critical component of the process of materializing a successful outcome. Key internal motivators such as a feeling of accomplishment, being energized, fit, sexy, attractive, happy and confidant can drive you to great success.

"I love to go to the beach and want to feel good in a bathing suit" can motivate one at any age. "I want to play with my kids". "I want to be pain free and enjoy a vacation with my family". These are all powerful motivational statements.

EXTERNAL MOTIVATORS

External motivators are also powerful. Common examples: "I have a class reunion coming up, a wedding, a cruise, or a birthday with a zero at the end of it". Wherever you get motivation from, there is always a driving mental force and thought process repeating that consequently evokes a change in behavior. If we go back to the "why" we are taking action, the new behavioral path is reinforced and materializes with ease. This is an example of quantum physics at it's best.

Here are a few examples of strong motivators:

» Feeling energized
» High self esteem
» Looking fit
» Decrease pain or becoming pain free
» Sense of well-being
» Increase confidence
» Inner peace
» Happiness
» Optimal health
» Decrease or discontinue medications
» Resolve health issues
» Quality time with family and friends
» Reduce and alleviate stress
» Optimal rest
» A sense of accomplishment
» Being a great role model
» Attracting new relationships
» Success within your career
» Vibrant presence
» Wearing a smaller size
» A vacation

» A birthday
» A wedding
» A class or family reunion

CREATING CHANGE
Before you can make significant changes in your life, it is important that you understand your current story. The best way to create lasting change is to understand where you are starting and clearly understand where you are going. We will explore where you can go in later chapters, but first let us talk about your starting point.

WHAT TO DO
1. Spend a few minutes in a quiet room. Sit quietly and reflect on where you are right now in your life.

I am _____

I see _____

I feel _____

I am _____

I want _____

I understand _____

I try _____

I am _____

I say _____

I do _____

I do not _____

I am _____

2. Fill in the blanks below with the words that best describe where you are right now.
3. Review what you just wrote. Place a star beside the things that you are happy or satisfied with. Place an X beside the things that you are dissatisfied with.
4. Put your story up in a place where you can see it every day – your bathroom mirror or your refrigerator.

5. Your Food

The A-B-Cs: Principle A = All low glycemic meals

My best definition of Low Glycemic is a meal that is devoid of starch and sugar.

What I can say with confidence is that meals that have no starch and sugar will surely make you lean. To take that one step further, the numbers never lie. If you eat the low glycemic, balanced meals I lay out as a baseline for your nutrition, you will burn fat with ease and never re-gain excess body fat.

I've trained and coached hundreds of clients and many health and fitness professionals on nutrition for success. The formula always works.

The numbers never lie. If you eat meals based on a serving of protein, combined with fiber and some healthy fat, your body will burn fat. It has been proven, yet so many nutrition plans fall short of coming back to this baseline.

If you eat meals with a full serving of grains and sugars of any type, those meals will cause your insulin to spike and hold up your fat-burning progress. You cannot keep spiking insulin with sugar and starch daily and keep burning fat. I'm going to keep the technical information out of this book and share the simple secrets to success.

Stop eating grains. Yes, on the whole, I recommend getting off bread, pasta and cereal as staples in the diet. Follow these simple things you can do which will be your secrets to success:

» Stop eating sugar.
» Stop eating starch.
» Eat protein every meal.
» Eat fiber every meal.
» Eat some healthy fat at every meal.
» Never eat carbohydrates without a serving of protein.
» Stop buying processed foods.
» Look at your food and understand the source and quality of each food.
» Know what effect food has on your body and how meals affect your blood sugar levels.

The above topics all play a part in simply being lean. I'll go in to what they mean and how they have a materializing effect. Much of this ties into the low glycemic meals, food choices and the consciousness piece of simply burning fat.

CARBOHYDRATES – THE REAL STORY!
Understanding carbohydrate consumption is critical to success. There is a mass of confusion and misinformation in this area of nutrition.

Carbohydrates defined – An organic compound comprising of carbon, hydrogen and oxygen.

Carbohydrates are sugars that vary in composition and the way they impact blood sugar. This program is built on consuming carbohydrates predominantly from green and yellow vegetables. When consumed, these vegetables create the slowest rise in blood sugar. A slow rise in blood sugar is important, as it make easy for your body to burn fat.

NELSONS' STORY
Nelson's trainer, Randy, referred Nelson to me for nutritional counseling due to his inability to control his blood sugar readings. Nelson had been diagnosed as a type 1 diabetic 5 years earlier. The cause of the onset of his diabetes is unknown.

During the initial assessment, Nelson reported he was experiencing low and high blood sugar readings regularly. His wife attended the intake session and was quite attentive and supportive. She told me that he would consume excessive amounts of sweets and high carbohydrate foods if they were available. Nelson said he would have high blood sugar readings regularly – periodically, his blood sugar spiked to more than 400.

Nelson also knew that he needed to lose excess body fat. His skin tone appeared to be a bit sallow. He enjoyed his workouts but the low blood sugar readings were problematic. When I asked Nelson what he typically ate before his workouts, his answer was "a bagel". I also discovered that he did not eat enough protein and relied heavily on grains and fruit as a high percentage of his daily food intake. He did eat meals consistently at the same time every day.

My prescription to Nelson was the following:

Give up grains altogether to stabilize blood sugar and reduce body fat percentage.

» Consume 20 to 35 grams of protein each meal. All proteins should be complete proteins.
» Each meal is to consist of protein, five or more grams of healthy fat and five, or more grams of fiber.
» Time all meals within three hours of each other.
» Eat six meals per day.

Within 4 weeks Nelson had not had a single low blood sugar reading. After adding a serving fiber to each meal his high blood sugar readings were the lowest they had been since becoming a type 1 diabetic.

On our third session, it was apparent that eating fruit (an apple) without protein resulted in an insulin spike of 180. After 4 sessions of keeping a food journal and engaging in nutrition counseling, Nelson lost 7lbs in 30 days and regulated his blood sugar levels. He had also adapted his eating patterns for extended business travel and was able to maintain his blood sugar levels consistently.

On our 4th session we tested Nelson's body fat percentage and determined he would lose an additional 7lbs. His total weight loss would be 14lbs. Nelson was expected to continue his progress and be totally successful controlling his blood sugar levels ongoing.

Nelson's comments on points that made the biggest difference for success:

» Give up grains
» Track all meals
» Fruits were to be consumed sparingly with protein
» Add fiber to each meal to avoid insulin spikes
» Body fat dropped naturally with attention to diet

The next main question is how to define low glycemic meals? Truthfully, my definition is going to be a **whole lot different** than much of the current literature. The simple fat burn definition is one that does not spike insulin. The food combining is critical to success. I'll first go into detail about the meals, and later entertain the numbers behind the formula that works consistently.

Protein from a viable source is the base of each meal. Yes,

even for those who "don't like to eat meat." Yes, even for those who are vegan and vegetarian. It works. Part of the reason we know this works is the numbers attributed to the glycemic index that correlate with the balanced meals. Nelson's case is an excellent example of success through re-configuring his meals. Hundreds of successful clients support the science of balancing blood sugar through nutrition. Various successful nutrition plans have demonstrated this. Learning what works and why it works is critical to ongoing success.

6. Movement

EXERCISE!

Move your body daily because all exercise is beneficial. By far, the most effective exercise that results in fat burning is strength training. Strength training is defined as moving your muscles with bodyweight and/or exercise equipment. As a trainer for 17 years, I highly recommend strength training three times a week and adding cardiovascular exercise.

Cardiovascular exercise is defined as running, biking, swimming, group exercise classes and using other cardiovascular equipment such as an elliptical machine that elevates the heart rate. Cardiovascular exercise can be combined with strength training in a workout.

The amount of exercise and intensity you participate in depends on your capabilities, level of fitness and desired outcome. Consult with a fitness professional for an appropriate exercise prescription.

7. Consciousness

THINK!

Consciousness refers to your level of awareness, focus, participation and engagement. The more you focus on low glycemic, balanced meals, the faster your results are obtained. Being vigilant of portions, engaging in tracking and knowing you are changing habits permanently materializes results.

GET YOUR TEAM TOGETHER

Share your desires for creating fitness with your family, friends, mentors, trainer and coach. Engaging others and making them aware of your ideal outcome, and this can be a powerful way to ensure ongoing success.

ENSURE FAT BURNING WITH EVERY MEAL

Here's How you do it:
» Define your targets for fat loss and track progress.
» Eat 6 meals per day.

» Log everything in your food journal and follow the plan with accountability (accountability is simply a series of corrections.)

» Have an accountability partner.

» Think "whole foods" Examples: olives, apples, and almonds.

» You can trade the protein choices in the example menu for any lean protein – examples are: meat, fish, eggs, high protein shake, edamame or turkey.

» Buy organic meats and eggs, when possible.

» Yogurt must be organic Greek PLAIN sweetened with stevia. (The yogurts with fruit added are full of sugar; do not eat these for fat loss.)

» Whey protein shakes are great for fat burning. Protein shakes must be low-carb (4 or less) and at least 20 grams of protein per serving.

» Cut out sugar and starch from your diet, read all labels, looking for hidden sugar. Bread, pasta, rice, cookies, crackers, cakes, chips and various processed snacks must be avoided on a daily basis. Fruit should be eaten sparingly and ONLY post-workout.

» Log all your food in a journal. Write in the time, content and quantity.

» Don't forget your water! It's your FAT LOSS liquid. For smaller women I recommend 80 ounces (2.5 quarts) of fluids per day. And for men of medium to larger build a gallon of fluids per day. You can count shakes, tea and coffee.

» Hire a professional trainer or coach, as you'll make more rapid progress.

» Schedule your workouts every week with your trainer and on your own.

» Make your program FUN...enjoy and celebrate your success!

PART III:
Your Food

8. Insulin And Blood Sugar

CONTROL IS CRITICAL TO SUCCESS

Getting lean, healthy and slowing the aging process is certainly a game of controlling blood sugar levels. Insulin is the hormone responsible for blood sugar levels. When a personal training or nutrition client comes to me wanting to lose body fat, I listen to them describe their diet and I am checking for foods and meals that spike insulin. I then, find the blood sugar spikes, make the corrections, and the client becomes lean quickly!

Remember that Ideal blood sugar levels are 70-120.

If you eat one cracker or a cookie, your blood sugar could spike somewhere between 100-150.

During my first year working in fitness, one of my personal trainers told me, "Eat a potato and you are eating a bowl of sugar." I recently talked to a diabetic client, who after eating a piece of cake tested her blood sugar at 325. Certainly the biggest issue in losing body fat is one that the average overweight person clearly fails to understand. Medical professionals and personal trainers also can benefit greatly from understanding the role blood sugar levels play in health conditions and the reduction of body fat percentage.

One of my clients said, "If I don't keep the food log, you can't help me." After a year of nutrition counseling, coaching and personal training, she is getting it! She's lost 15lbs and is on the path to losing more.

Carbohydrates are very simple to understand – green and yellow vegetables are the fibrous carbohydrate. They are excellent for you. Non-fibrous carbohydrates such as potatoes, rice, corn and processed foods spike blood sugar and promote fat storage. Grains are very high glycemic. Thus, I believe in a diet with little to no grains for those looking to burn body fat.

Processed foods such as bread, cereals, crackers, cookies, cakes, pies, pretzels, potato chips, alcohol and juice should be consumed sparingly or not at all. I spell them out here because these foods frequently get overlooked. We make excuses and tell ourselves, "it's really not that much, and it's only once in a while." However, disease and high body fat percentages persist.

When asking clients about their diet, I am checking for spikes in insulin. Once we correct and balance the blood sugar levels we can create a healthy, lean client. Yes, that's what I really do as a personal trainer!

Fruit is a mixed bag in terms of keeping insulin levels stable. Strawberries, are one of the highest antioxidant foods, however, they are composed of sugar. Strawberries should be eaten with a serving of protein such as with a tuna salad. Fruit, in general, should be consumed in small amounts and only after a workout for fat burning. Eating an apple without pairing it with protein can spike insulin to 180.

The issue with eating non-fibrous carbohydrates and processed foods is that we consume too much, too frequently. You'd be surprised how very little processed food, non-fibrous carbohydrates and/or fruit it takes to increase insulin levels. Depending on the content, it's not much!

When insulin increases and blood sugar numbers are 150 and higher on a daily basis you just get fatter, hungrier and exhausted. Frequent spikes promote fat storage, increased body fat and a multitude of other serious health issues. The main issues are heart disease, high cholesterol, inflammatory disorders, hormonal disorders, lethargy, anxiety and depression.

Question:
Short of managing and testing blood sugar levels daily, how do I keep it balanced?

Answer:
» Follow the menus and options in the Simple Fat Burn examples.

» Become highly conscious and aware of what you are eating and how you feel before, during and after your meals.
» Stop buying processed foods at the grocery store...trust me, if they are in the house, you will eat them!
» Keep a food log.
» Pay attention to the timing of your meals.
» Work with an accountability partner! Another person is your best and strongest connection to facilitate a true, consistent change in habits.
» Eat a serving of protein (20-40 grams) at every mini meal (6X per day).

Balance your blood sugar by getting focused on what you are eating, one meal at a time. Stop eating too much fruit, processed foods and non-fibrous vegetables as staples in the diet. Disease will diminish, if not disappear. Body fat will decrease, and you will feel amazing.

Simple Fat Burn Concept: If you want to change your life, change your nutrition.

9. The Numbers Never Lie

Here is the formula to burn fat and keeping your blood sugar balanced. Hit this target for all 6 meals per day.

20 – 40 grams Protein, 5 grams Fat, 5+ grams Fiber = Fat Burning

A petite to medium sized woman would consume 20-30 grams of protein per mini meal. A medium – large male would consume 30-40 grams of protein per mini meal. A male who desires to build mass would consume 50 grams of protein 6-7X per day. This is not a "high protein diet". It's a mathematical calculation based on size, adequate protein intake and tangible outcome. Your cells are made of protein, and it is the building block of lean muscle.

SIMPLE FAT BURN

Simple Fat Burn Concept: Never eat a carbohydrate (fruit or vegetable) without a full serving of protein. This is critical for success.

This is the formula for the Simple Fat Burn meals that keep insulin at an appropriate level thus allowing the body to burn fat naturally. When you add daily exercise, you can create an effective prescription for becoming and being fit and lean for life.

Examples of simple fat burn meals:
» Grilled chicken and salad
» Protein shake (add fiber) and almonds
» Omelet with vegetables (4+ egg whites and one yolk)
» Fish and a green vegetable
» Edamame salad
» Steak and salad
» Tuna salad over a green salad
» Deviled eggs and cut vegetables
» Lettuce wraps with turkey and avocado

Grains, bread, rice and cereal are specifically omitted, as they are detrimental to weight loss. The one word to understand in the fat-burning process is INSULIN. Insulin is simply defined as the hormone produced by the pancreas that is responsible for fat and carbohydrate metabolism in the body. When insulin levels run high (with consumption of starch and sugars) insulin stops the use of fat as an energy source.

SIMPLE FAT BURN

What you need to know for success:

» Blood sugar levels simply rise too high with consumption of starch and sugar. Therefore fat burning is essentially halted. It takes very little starch and/or sugar to do this. One cracker can spike insulin 6 points. Most people over-consume processed and packaged foods due to a spike in insulin.

» Fruit is included in the shopping list. Only the lowest sugar fruits are included.

» You may have days that you eat zero fruit; this may accelerate progress for fat burning.

» Once per day or less, is the maximum frequency for consuming fruit for fat burning.

» Consume fruit ONLY post-workout for fat burning.

» The best sweeteners are stevia, xylitol and sorbitol.

WHAT TO DO
Follow these steps to start seeing success today

1. Keep a food log or nutrition journal.
2. Have an accountability partner (or several).
3. Keep high glycemic foods and processed foods out of the house.
4. Make a master grocery list and schedule shopping and cooking.
5. Delegate tasks so that healthy food is always available. You may need help with preparation and cooking. Or you may need to delegate other tasks so you can shop and prepare food.

6. Be prepared with several meals when you leave home for the day.
7. Talk to others and share your experiences and challenges.
8. Continue learning and strategizing for success.
9. Be aware of both your strengths and weaknesses with your personal plan.
10. Try new recipes. Keep your meals interesting with spices and garnishes.

10. The Food Plan

The Sample Nutrition plans are meant as a guide or roadmap. This is not a "diet plan" but is to be used as a blueprint for building your own nutrition plan. The protein and carbohydrate ratios are configured to burn fat. You can use any of the protein sources interchangeably throughout a given day. The key is for women to eat 20-30 grams of protein per meal, and men averaging 30-40 grams per meal.

Fruit should be included once per day (or less for weight loss) and only post-workout paired with a protein. This is the correct configuration to keep insulin from spiking and to promote fat burning. Low glycemic meals are defined as those that burn fat, as opposed to storing fat.

SIMPLE FAT BURN

SAMPLE DAILY NUTRITION PLAN FOR WOMEN

Breakfast
- » 1 Egg plus 3 egg whites - use organic eggs!
- » ¼ cup of blueberries or mixed berries - frozen or fresh (optional), 1 packet stevia
- » OR Vegetable Omelet (one egg plus 3 egg whites)
- » OR – Protein shake
- » Multivitamin, EFA's (2 capsules essential fatty acids), fiber supplement

Meal #2 – Mid morning
- » Protein shake and 12-20 Almonds
- » OR – Quest bar

Lunch
- » 3 - 5 oz chicken breast (grilled, baked or broiled) or white fish
- » 1 cup fresh green salad
- » Green vegetable
- » 1 tbsp extra-virgin olive oil or flaxseed oil, 1 tbsp vinegar (any)
- » 1 cup green tea (optional)

Meal#4 - Afternoon
- » Fish, (suggest - tuna) or chicken and a green salad
- » OR Protein shake
- » 1 tablespoon ground flax, fiber supplement

Dinner

» 3 - 4 oz salmon or white fish (grilled, baked, or broiled) or shrimp
» 1 cup steamed vegetables
» EFA"s (essential fatty acids) (2 capsules)
» ¼ - 1/2 grapefruit (citrus for fat-burning)
» Fiber supplement

Meal #6 - Evening

» Protein shake or any other source of protein (fish, chicken), fiber supplement
» Tea of your choice

SAMPLE DAILY NUTRITION PLAN FOR MEN

Breakfast

» 1 Egg plus 6 egg whites -OR- vegetable omelet
» OR – Protein shake
» 2 capsules Omega-3 fish oil (EFA's)
» Fiber supplement

Meal #2 – Mid-morning

» Protein shake and 1 cup berries or green apple (fruit is optional, best used post-workout).
» ¼ cup Almonds or walnuts
» OR – Quest bar

SIMPLE FAT BURN

Lunch
» 6 - 8 oz Chicken breast (grilled, baked or broiled) -OR- white fish -OR- salmon
» 2 cups Green salad
» 1 tbsp Extra-virgin olive oil or flaxseed oil
» 1 tbsp Vinegar
» 1 cup green tea (optional)

Meal #4 - afternoon
» Protein shake or protein choice of any kind
» Vegetables (optional)
» ¼ cup Almonds or walnuts

Dinner
» 6 - 8 oz Chicken, salmon – OR - any fish (grilled, baked, or broiled) , -OR- lean organic beef
» 1 cup Steamed vegetables & salad
» 1 Grapefruit (optional)

Meal #6 - evening
» Protein shake or protein of any kind
» 1/4 cup Almonds or walnuts
» Tea of your choice

VEGETARIAN OPTIONS
The vegetarian options for protein as the base of the meal are:

» Eggs
» Edamame

» Protein shakes (low carb – 4 or less)
» TVP – textured vegetable protein (added to soups or vegetables)
» Tofu
» Tempeh
» Quest protein bar – The only approved bars
» Cottage cheese (may not work well for some individuals)
» Greek yogurt (organic, plain) (may not work well for some individuals).

THE SIMPLE FAT BURN FORMULA

The ideal balance within each meal for protein, fat, carbohydrates and fiber:

» 20-40 grams of **protein** (depending on male or female and the size of the person)
» 5 grams of healthy **fat**
» 5-8 grams of **fiber** (or more)
» No Sugar or low Sugar 3 grams (or less)
» 10 or fewer grams of carbohydrates

Simple Fat Burn Concept: Spiking insulin and going longer than 3 hours without eating are the causes of gaining and storing excess body fat.

Vegetables are appropriate for consumption and they **are carbohydrates.** Thus re-defining, the loose paradigm of "low-carb" is necessary for success. Our scientific approach is "low glycemic", NOT to be confused with the "low-carb" definition. After years of watching clients test their blood sugar, it's clear that starch and sugar drastically spike insulin. It's unreasonable to include such items as bread, pasta and rice as staples in a permanent fat-burning nutrition plan.

Simple Fat Burn is not a "low-carb" plan. It is extremely misleading to define a nutrition plan as "low carb", when foods that spike insulin promote fat storage. Many popular diets and nutrition plans allow for grains and processed foods, thus making long-term success impossible.

Net carbs are the number of carbohydrates to watch per meal and per day. Net carbs are carbohydrates minus the fiber and any sugar alcohols (stevia, xylitol, maltitol are sweeteners that will not spike insulin when used sparingly). If a salad has 8 carbs and 4 grams of fiber, the net carbs are 4 for the salad.

When net carbs are 25 or less per day, one can expect to burn fat consistently at an accelerated rate.

11. Shopping And Organizing

I am a list maker. I make lists on paper, on whiteboards and on my phone. I love to make a list for the day and take it to the store. I have a list in marker on my bathroom mirror. What better place to jot things down as you think of them?

Simple Fat Burn Concept: Organization is the key to success – maybe even the key to sanity.

I love to make a master list of all my favorite recipes, staples in my healthy diet, and my son's favorite meals.

When a demanding schedule permits for little time for shopping and cooking, organizing is the key. You may pick up some healthy options at your favorite restaurant. I'm a big fan of getting salads, organic vegetables and lean protein to go. Having a freezer stocked with meats, fish and organic frozen vegetables can be critical to success. It only takes a few minutes to thaw and cook a healthy meal.

Delegation of tasks, shopping, and food preparation may be critical to your success. The other option is to delegate other household tasks so that you have time and energy to shop and cook. However you configure the execution of your own Simple Fat Burn strategy, someone has to make the highest standard of food available to you. This does take some actual planning and "time on task" each week.

Be sure to ask family members to help. If they do not oblige, **continue with your strategy**. I've often had personal assistants and childcare help that could assist with errands and food preparation. A little bit of focused help goes a long way and is extremely appreciated!

EXAMPLE FOOD/SHOPPING LIST

» The best sweeteners are stevia, xylitol, sorbitol and maltitol. Consume sweeteners sparingly.

» Always choose from the protein list FIRST to build a meal. Never eat carbohydrates without a full serving of protein.

» Use the last column of spices combined with a garnish of fruit to give meals color and favor. This will keep your healthy meals colorful, interesting and appetizing. A few berries and pecans added to a grilled chicken salad make an incredible difference.

» *Consume sweet potatoes in a small amount and preferably after a workout. They are a higher carbohydrate food and can spike insulin. Sweet potatoes are a root vegetable, not comparable to a white potato, which is very high glycemic.

Protein	Carbohydrates	Fats	Spices
Bison	Apple	Almonds	Basil
Chicken Breast	Asparagus	Avocado	Cacao
Crab	Bell Pepper	Bacon	Celery Seed
Eggs	Blueberries	Butter	Cilantro
Edamame	Broccoli	Cashews	Cinnamon
Ground Beef (lean)	Carrots	Coconut Oil	Cumin
Ground Turkey (lean)	Celery	Olive Oil	Curry Powder
Grouper	Cherries	Pecans	Garlic
Haddock	Cucumber	Pistachios	Ginger
Pork Chop	Green Beans	Sesame Oil	Grill Seasoning
Pork Roast	Green Onions	Walnuts	Jalapenos
Protein Shake	Jicama	Walnut Oil	Lemon
Quest Bar	Kale		Lime
Red Snapper	Leeks		Mrs. Dash
Salmon Filet	Lettuce		Mint
Sausage (lean)	Onion		Paprika
Scallops	Orange		Rosemary
Shrimp	Pears		Sage
Steak	Raspberries		Salsa
Tofu	Squash		Tarragon

SIMPLE FAT BURN

Protein	Carbohydrates	Fats	Spices
Tuna	Spinach		Thyme
Turkey Breast	Squash		Vinegar
TVP*	Strawberries		
	Sweet Potatoes		
	Tomatoes		
	Zucchini		

*TVP – Textured vegetable protein is dehydrated soy protein.

PART IV:
Movement

12. Your Body In Motion

I spent the first ten years of my career as a fitness trainer focusing on exercise and learning the technical part of how to work out effectively to get maximum results in minimal time. The body must be challenged on a regular basis to provoke a positive physiological response. Exercise is critical to optimal health. Although it is possible to burn fat and lose excess weight without exercise, it is simply not an ideal long-term plan for peak performance and increased energy. Strength training, in particular, and exercises that improve core strength, are highly recommended and encouraged.

Cardiovascular exercise is complementary and part of a well-balanced fitness regimen. Additional components of agility, balance, and flexibility are also addressed in a comprehensive fitness program. The best way to address each component of your fitness program is with the guidance of an experienced professional personal trainer.

SIMPLE FAT BURN

I've hired and learned from more than 20 top personal trainers. I've been the trainee and student throughout my entire personal training career. There is no substitute for a personal prescription for health and fitness. Two minds working together to evoke a positive change is powerful. I do caution people to be "free agent-thinkers" listen to your body, your intuition, and your gut instinct when working with any professional.

Simple Fat Burn Concept: Your body will tell you everything you need to know. Just slow down and listen.

Being pain free is a part of physical fitness that is often segregated or altogether bypassed. I have at times, over-trained and suffered injuries, strains and various painful conditions. I have had pain in my knees, back, elbows, wrist, bicep, hip, and the worst were various problems with my feet. Today I am pain free.

The key concepts to being and staying pain free involve listening to the body, balanced nutrition, alignment of the musculoskeletal system and training appropriately. A few years ago, I was introduced to an incredible methodology that reduces pain thorough postural alignment exercises.

My friend Kathy Mulherin taught me to prescribe exercise to reduce pain for various conditions. I learned that through education and resources, pain that occurs in the joints or muscles could often be reduced and often alleviated with exercises and stretches for alignment. A low glycemic diet is also critical to being pain free. The simple fat burn nutrition concepts reduce inflammation within the body. Between practicing balanced nutrition and postural exercises, one can drastically reduce and often entirely alleviate pain.

At 44 years old, I am in athletic condition. I can sprint, run, lift heavy weights, and have zero pain in any part of my body. Exercise and nutrition are the mental and physical medicine the body needs on a daily basis. If you would like to learn more about pain relief through exercise, go to: http://postureandfunction. com.

I once was told that a bottle of medicine can kill you, but the appropriate dose holds the cure. That holds true with exercise. It is important to understand the amount and intensity of exercise that works for you. The amount of exercise I typically recommend for the average person to engage in is 3 to 7 hours of exercise per week. For a strong baseline that promotes fitness and energy, focus on resistance training and cardiovascular exercises.

My ideal exercise week looks like:

» 3-4 strength training sessions (45-60 minutes) working various muscle groups or circuit training (all muscle groups in one workout)
» 2-4 cardiovascular sessions – walking hills, sprints, getting outside (30-60 minutes)

SIMPLE FAT BURN

This is an ideal plan. Over the years my plan has changed to include intense strength training with split routines, cardio-kickboxing, spin classes, martial arts, running and intense strength and conditioning sessions.

One concept I frequently refer to is that **change** within your routines, style and the execution of your workouts is important. Your exercise routine should be challenging and change you both mentally and physically. Sticking with one simple routine for years on end is the least productive way to evoke a positive physiological and psychological response. For most people, change is the ticket that works. However, if you have a solid plan that is working, stick with it. I have been consistent on one format at times for years, and it served me well.

Your ideal personal plan most likely looks a lot different from mine. However, the components of strength training that encompass moving your muscles, while incorporating core strength movements will greatly assist the fat burning process. The component of cardiovascular exercise (getting the heart rate elevated) is the other critical component of any successful fitness program.

PART V:
Consciousness

13. Consciousness For Success

This is probably the most understated and overlooked principal in most nutrition and fitness programs. Quite simply, it's the fact that what you think, say and feel about your fitness, health, and well-being drives your success.

Understanding all of the content in this program is only the beginning. Thinking successfully, speaking the truth of transformation and feeling lean, fit and energized, is truly the key to manifesting long-term change. You must become your new self – a self that eats low-glycemic, balanced meals, exercises consistently, and knows you are lean permanently.

When you can accept that the old way is over and the new way is a state of being, you are on your road to success. You burn fat with every meal. You exercise most days effectively and efficiently. You are a new and healthier version of yourself.

Consciousness is:

» Your thoughts that encompass feelings and lead to actions.
» A place of complete understanding that is highly aware, engaged and productive.
» Something that can be shared when someone asks for accurate information.
» A way of being that makes sense and always works – it is in alignment with your values.
» Awareness that comes from a place of knowing and is always offered with compassion.
» A critical piece of your success.
» Tied to core beliefs that you may, or may not, be fully aware of.
» The sum total of your feelings, beliefs and actions that create your experience.

Consciousness in terms of spirituality:

Consciousness is probably one of my favorite topics and tools to use in this and any other transformative program or prescription. This program is meant for all people of all religions and backgrounds.

Addictions are healed every day through consciousness and support systems. There is a spiritual and emotional component to health and healing. Bringing in the personal spiritual belief infrastructure that works for you is a powerful and critical for success. It is important that we not judge others and ourselves for shortcomings but instead assist and believe we can elevate our standards.

SIMPLE FAT BURN

Simple Fat Burn Concept: When you have a higher understanding, you are called to conduct yourself in a manner that is in alignment with that information.

Effective options for elevating consciousness

Powerful options for excelling at the consciousness part of this program are:

» Meditation
» Prayer
» Scripting
» Visualization

Wherever you are on your personal path of spiritual awareness and development these options will serve you well in making progress exponentially. Just reading this book can have an effect of reassuring you that change is not only possible, but also probable.

14. Just Lighten Up!

Let me tell you about the day we had drinks at the gym. Please know that this was an isolated incident. One day we were talking about trips to Epcot Center in Florida and all the interesting restaurants with multicultural foods and experiences. The consensus was that the frozen Grand Marnier orange slush drinks were notably the best part of Epcot.

The next week, Arlene came in to her training session with a "surprise" fresh pitcher of frozen Grand Marnier Orange Slush drinks, "with just a little alcohol" for everyone in the training studio to sample. After about 20 minutes we were all joking, tipsy and laughing hysterically. One of the clients (Kim) plopped down in the office chair and proclaimed, "I'm drunk!" I still laugh about the day we had Orange Slush drinks at the gym. We laughed so hard we cried. My point here is that having fun is critical to success, even if it means derailing a workout now and then. It's well worth it.

SIMPLE FAT BURN

I think the topics of fitness and weight loss have to be taken lightly in order for people to stick with it, to progress, and to get and stay engaged with the process. We all need to be less serious while simultaneously getting focused and materializing results. If creating fitness has an element of fun, we will come back and tell others to join us. Don't we all remember the days and times when we had **the most fun** in an activity, a trip, a workshop, or relationship?

Simple Fat Burn Concept: Create a culture that is fun and engaging.

When I worked with my first trainer at Bally's Total Fitness we talked a lot. J.D. was my mentor, friend and teacher. I still remember him telling me "When you cheat, you only cheat yourself." Those words still ring in my ears. Not only did I lose all the fat and work my body like never before, what I remember the most is that we laughed. And we laughed a lot while I transformed from overweight to fit.

There are characters in every fitness scene that make for great stand-up comedy. There was a man who wrapped up his barbell (loaded with hundreds of pounds) in paper towels. Then lifted it a total of 4 inches and repeatedly dropped it. Actually, it was more like slammed it on the rack several times. I found this extremely disruptive.

I can remember J.D. shaking his head at this "interesting technique." As a former bodybuilder, trainer and Chiropractor, he wanted to say, "Sir, after 24 years in the gym, I have never seen this weightlifting technique. What are you doing?" This was probably the most unproductive, disruptive, self-made, heavy weight-lifting technique ever witnessed in the gym.

There was the mother who wanted me to make her daughter taller. Yes, I had heard her correctly. She had me on the phone for over 20 minutes. She was talking "at me", about Sophie, her teenage daughter, (my new client) who she wanted me to make taller. I gently explained that we did not have exercises to make her taller. We (the front desk and management staff) joked, "We have the stretcher out back".

I've met some really interesting people who helped me along the way as a trainer. Jon Benedict was a former personal trainer who had trained a football team. Jon honestly had the best, most muscular legs I have ever seen on a man in the gym. Early in my training career, Jon was my mentor, friend, and training partner. One day I confessed I had long been neglecting to train my shoulders. I hated, **just plain hated** to train them. Why? Because they were weak and it was so hard.

Jon asked me this question: "What is it going to take to get you to train shoulders?" Done. Today I love to train shoulders. If there were any body part I could actually describe as "craving" to train today, it would be shoulders. Hence, further proof that **people really can change.**

SIMPLE FAT BURN

At another point, and this was one of many various conversations with several diverse professionals over the years, I confessed to Jon I was really struggling **again** with my diet. Here came Jon's life changing question, "What is it going to take to get you to clean up your diet?" I immediately embraced his nutrition suggestions, created structure, got focused and made improvements. Great trainers, coaches and counselors ask the right questions.

Jon had a favorite training story that he loved to tell again and again. Jon was a personal trainer and he had a client named Amy. Yes, I even remember her name, as the client who had made the rounds using every personal trainer in the gym and got minimal results. She drove Jon and everyone else crazy with endless questions and lack of compliance. One day she asked Jon "what is it going to take for me to lose 20lbs by the end of the month?" Jon told her to "Cut off your right leg." Amy ran off crying. Jon was severely reprimanded by management. Jon loved to tell his best personal training story laughing his way through it.

Almost every trainer who has worked in the field for years has the "dropped their drawers story". We routinely do a three site skinfold test to measure body fat composition. Using calipers we pinch the skinfolds, add up the factors and tell the client where their body fat percentage is currently and determine a target in the "good or excellent range". Johnny was a short, muscular body builder who asked me to test his body fat one day. We're back in my office and as I am getting out the calipers

I hear Johnny say "I hope you're not shy 'cause I'm sure not." As I turned around I now see Johnny is in his underwear!

I yelled "Nooooo, that's not necessary!" As I was covering my eyes, he got dressed, apologizing. I was holding my head with both hands, and was trying to regain my professional composure. I then completed the world's fastest body fat percentage test and moved on with my day thinking to myself, "This will never happen again."

I once had a sweet client named Anne in her mid 70's. Anne was an attractive, conservative, stylish southern belle. She had a husband who lived in an assisted living facility and she visited him regularly. When I did her initial assessment we were winding up our consultation in my office, I asked her if "There was anything else that was important to her in her health and fitness program?" She thought for a few moments and said with the utmost seriousness "A great sex life." There was no joking around on this one. I was so shocked I almost fell out of the chair! I took notes and concluded the consultation.

15. Accountability

Accountability here is defined as "A series of corrections"

The changes and main corrections in cleaning up your diet and structure to ignite the Simple Fat Burning process are the foundation for balancing blood sugar and controlling insulin levels. Your personal accountability helps to ensure that you are aware of the changes that you need to make and are consciously making those changes.

1. Stop eating bread, cereal, crackers, and desserts as staples in the diet.
2. Eating too much fruit and eating fruit by itself (without a protein).
3. Eating too little protein in a meal (example, two slices of turkey).
4. Skipping meals, (6 meals are ideal).
5. Grabbing nuts and calling them protein, does not make them a serving of protein.

6. Grazing on processed snack foods unconsciously (pretzels, crackers, cookies and candy).
7. Eating excessive amounts of nut butter.
8. Not drinking enough water daily.
9. Eating salads with high glycemic ingredients while dining out.
10. Eating sugar and bread and rationalizing it as "not a good day".
11. Ineffective and/or inconsistent exercise.
12. Inadequate fiber (less than 25 grams per day).
13. Eating too many protein bars and shakes, skipping real meals.
14. Neglecting to eat 3 or more servings of green vegetables daily.

Tools for accountability are aspects of your program that mark progress, increase awareness, and promote behavior modification. Choosing an accountability partner can provide you with another tool to help you realize great success with your health and fitness plan. I typically work with several accountability partners. An accountability partner can be anyone in your life who can help motivate you – a coach, a good friend, a spouse. The key is to find someone who supports your efforts.

Simple Fat Burn Concept: By accepting accountability, you are acknowledging that you are responsible for your actions.

Working with a great trainer or coach is surely the quickest path to success. The way in which your clothes fit, and how you look and feel are great markers of success. Yes, the scale is a productive tool to measure progress! The most successful clients weigh daily or at least weekly to correlate progress with actual trends in behavior. A food log or journal is your best means of tracking progress and closing the gap with unconscious decisions. When a professional looks at a food log, they are checking for trends and strategizing on how to assist the client in getting the job accomplished. This is quite an effective process to materialize an incredible change.

Accountability tools checklist:

- » Trainer and/or Coach
- » Accountability partner(s)
- » Food journal
- » Scale
- » Notes on how your clothes fit, how you look and feel
- » Measurements including body fat percentage
- » Medical test reports for comparison
- » Tracking systems
- » Written record of target weight/size
- » Progress pictures

PART VI:
Your New Story

16. Scripting – Writing Your New Story

The concept and practice of scripting has profoundly changed my life. I owe all the credit and thanks to Dr. Joyce Rennolds, "Motivator of one or a Thousand", and author of "The Energy Connection", for teaching the concept of scripting. I met Joyce while speaking at an event we hosted called "Total Woman Makeover." Joyce taught the power of writing your new story. She taught me to script, and I've been doing this daily for several years.

Scripting gives a powerful perspective on keeping a journal. The results that I, and thousands of others, have experienced from scripting have been absolutely outstanding. The scripting process is specific. You get a journal, a really nice journal, to use as your scripting book. This is important, as it is a reflection of your life that you are actively creating. You dedicate the journal to yourself and add in some specific details about what you value in this process.

In your journal you create the new story of your life, keeping the writing in the present tense, and writing as if it has already happened. It is important to write about what you are thankful for, express appreciation, and keep the content positive.

Scripting in specific detail works best. You are in fact, creating your new life as you write. You are scripting "new" desires, dreams, scenarios and your reality. Scripting is an action that results in a manifestation. You will find that the words you write show up in your life! I cannot express strongly enough the power of scripting.

This is such a simple practice that makes a massive difference in your health, relationships, finances, and every facet of life that you choose to focus on. Scripting is powerful and literally one of the best practices that I recommend engaging with on a daily basis. Script yourself lean, fit and incredibly healthy, amongst anything else your heart desires.

Here's an example:

Thank you for my extreme focus. I have clarity in my vision and purpose. My body is lean, toned, healthy and fit. My meals are healthy and balanced. I exercise daily and my results materialize with ease!

You can script for many things in life. In this context we apply scripting to health, fitness and body fat loss. You may script to be a specific size, weight, body fat percentage and/or toned areas of your body.

Another Example:

My body is lean, toned and I have flat abs. My arms are toned and sculpted. I have no excess fat on my body. My body fat percentage drops into the ideal range with ease. All my meals are low glycemic and I exercise daily. I am fully aware of my choices and decisions around food. I consistently practice eating meals that burn fat. I eat plenty of green vegetables and organic sources of protein. I am rested and have lots of energy!

17. Resources

Throughout your process, it is important that you find the resources that work well for you. Vitamins, supplements, protein powders, and protein bars can enhance your ability to burn fat and feel energized. Not every option works for everyone so you might need to try a few different types of products before you find what works best for you.

I have found these sites to provide a lot of great options:

» www.vitacost.com
» www.netrition.com
» www.bodybuilding.com – supplements, profiles, forums, workouts, and blogs.

SUPPLEMENTS FOR FAT-BURNING/ METABOLISM SUPPORT
Supplements are optional, but may greatly assist in the fat burning process and support metabolism.

» Multivitamin
» Fiber supplements
» Fish oil (EFA's) – liquid or capsules
» Vegetarian – EFA's, instead of fish oil
» CLA – Tonalin®
» Apple cider vinegar
» Green tea
» Cinnamon
» MCT oil – www.vitacost.com

PROTEIN BARS AND SHAKES

Protein bars and shakes are useful tools for fat loss and convenience. They are not the most natural source of nutrition, but can certainly help with the process. I recommend first making sure your shakes and bars do not have sugar in them. Next, I recommend using the highest quality shakes you can find. Stevia and the other sweeteners listed earlier would be the first pick as a sweetener in the shakes. There are a variety of products on the market.

Some of the best shakes I have used personally are:

» Blue Bonnet
» Betty Lou
» Optimal Nutrition – gold
» Bodylogix Natural Isolate
» Jay Robb
» Garden of Life

SIMPLE FAT BURN

You may find it most palatable to mix powder shakes with ice water, and unsweetened almond milk or unsweetened coconut milk. I typically blend my shakes with ice water and add fiber, as it is the quickest option. Protein shakes are always better quality in powder form than a ready to drink (RTD) shake. The RTD shake has a lower quality due to stabilizers that provide for a longer shelf life. However, a ready to drink shake is surely a better choice than a sandwich or fast food option, or even worse, skipping meals. I recommend getting off processed shakes when you have the time and resources to eat all natural foods.

Quest protein bars are Simple Fat Burn approved due to the exceptional quality of their all-natural line of protein bars. Quest bars contain 20 grams of protein, 17 grams of fiber (or more) and 4 net carbs. The numbers and taste are impressive. Please note: I am not paid to endorse any supplemental products.

Personally, I am not a purist when it comes to my own food choices. I do eat an occasional lower quality protein bar or shake. However, I do not eat fast food, bread, cookies or crackers as a "quick snack" or as staples in my diet. I've given up having processed crackers, cookies and cakes in the house. If I were to eat those very high carbohydrate options regularly as meals, I would gain fat and be VERY hungry within an hour after eating. I simply do not eat out of the pantry! High glycemic meals lend themselves to carb-cravings, over-calorizing, and rapid weight gain.

SIMPLE FAT BURN

Simple Fat Burn Concept: The flexibility and versatility of the Simple Fat Burn meals let you take the quality and convenience factors to the level that suits you personally.

When you spike insulin by eating high glycemic foods, the mind, body and spirit are all affected. When we eat low-glycemic meals (natural foods), and make the best quality choices, we are positively affected and feel so much better. Check in with how you are feeling with **each and every meal**. It's critical to your success.

Although bars and shakes can be useful tools for convenient mini-meals, keep in mind they are still processed food products. I recommend using them as much or as little as your lifestyle and comfort zone permits. You can certainly eat all natural meals, and many people do. Yes, it is possible in hectic, fast paced life to cook in batches, order salads and pick up great quality food for all meals.

ORGANIZATION:
MAKING YOUR PLAN WORK FOR EVERYDAY LIFE
Here are the top tips for organization of your personal plan:

» **Prioritize** – your outcome and activities that produce results.
» **Delegate** – as much as you can in all areas of life that you are comfortable passing off.
» **Create Systems** – organize for delegation and spending only the time that is necessary on each task.

- » **Batching** – cook in batches and make several meals at once.
- » **Master list** – Make your master list and keep it in your phone, kitchen or wherever you can easily access and utilize it.

18. Visualization

Visualization is a powerful technique for materializing your simple fat burn results. Many successful athletes use visualization as a tool for excelling at training and competition. Fitness competitors need to visualize what their physique will look like on the day of competition. Mental practice for actual competition is a critical piece of learning to get used to being in front of an audience with confidence and poise.

One of the most important tools any athlete can use before competing and during training for success is visualization. When I was competing in figure competitions my trainer, George Turmon told me to "think about what you want your body to look like on stage." I had to get a clear picture in my mind of what exactly I wanted my physique, stage presentation and presence to look like. I had to mentally create a clear picture of myself in the future through the process of visualization. This was some of the best advice I ever put into action to create a successful outcome.

SIMPLE FAT BURN

Not all of us process information visually, but I believe that this can be cultivated. If this speaks to you, use this tool consistently and you'll find the results are exponential. The visualization process is an incredible tool for those who are able to use it. Visualization can be done anywhere.

I process most of my daily information visually. For many of us, it's easy to create pictures in the mind. I can "see" most anything in my mind that I choose to focus on and visualize.

You may be a person who naturally processes information in terms of "feeling" a situation or outcome. I've found the best approach to success combines various aspects of visualization, feeling and auditory processing. The practice of visualizing your mental and physical state is clearly one that can, when practiced daily, play a huge role in the speed at which your results become reality.

The feeling, or kinesthetic process is strongest in the individual who processes by "feeling better" and uses this thought process and language to describe situations. We all have the capability to use this and develop it. A highly intuitive person may also be a visual processor. They may be in tune with all levels of processing information and pay particular attention to one more than others.

Simple Fat Burn Concept: Everything has a feeling to it. You just have to slow down and tune in to it.

I personally am an extremely visual person. I identify with physiological visual changes in others and myself first. In addition, I often describe the "feeling space" of programs, people and events. Often people ask me "what are you talking about"? If you have a friend with a troubling situation you can intuitively "feel" that person is stressed, anxious, worried or depressed. Although you may have strong visual and kinesthetic perception, the auditory processing component is also critical to effective communication. We all need to be GREAT listeners!

19. Meditation

One of the most powerful tools you can use in the process of getting healthy, lean and fit is meditation. The process of quieting the mind for a few minutes is truly priceless when it comes to transformation. To define meditation, I asked author of "Chasin' Meditation", Christopher "Chase" Carey, MBA to provide clarity. "What Meditation Is: Meditation is being in an Expanded State of Awareness with a quieted mind and body. We quiet the mind and body through physical and mental exercises. We meditate to change our external world."

As a person who frequently takes the shortest path to obtain the fastest result, meditation strikes me as a methodology that provides immediate, consistent results for those who practice it. There are many benefits to breathing, quieting and focusing the mind. In the orient, the racing, unfocused mind is called the Monkey Mind. This is frequently a problem with getting enough rest. A person goes to bed tired, and although they should be falling asleep, the Monkey Mind keeps them awake.

SIMPLE FAT BURN

Your fitness transformation experience offers a great opportunity to begin practicing meditation. Most likely you will fall asleep when your body needs sleep. Rest is an extremely important phase of health, fitness and mental focus. I have found that a few minutes of meditation per day can produce restfulness equivalent to several hours of sleep. That is priceless!

Meditation can be focused on or around any area of life that needs healing. Often compulsive behaviors, disease and health disorders are alleviated and healed through meditation. Through the process of quieting the mind, you can truly move rapidly to higher levels of functioning in a very short time. A few minutes spent weekly or daily can produce a wealth of inner peace, calmness and productivity.

There are many formats for meditation. Group meditation, individual, guided, or simply listening to music or quietly focusing on the breath are all options to begin. One of the simplest ways to meditate is to scan the internet for short meditations and see what strikes your interest. This can be done any time of the day that works for you. Here's a simple strategy: take a workday afternoon break and listen to a 10 minute meditation on YouTube. Sitting in a quiet space breathing for a few minutes a day can change one's life immensely.

Classes, videos and CD's are all useful tools to create a meditative practice. Once the results of meditation are experienced, one can become highly motivated to regularly engage in meditation daily. The benefits are exponential. Meditation is well worth the investment of time and focus.

20. Prayer

Prayers can be written, silent, verbal and shared with others or kept to your self. If you have a religion, religious practice, or interest in this area of your life, I encourage you to bring this into your transformation process. I've often put others and myself on prayer lists. You can easily find prayer lists online. In many situations I have e-mailed my personal contacts asking for prayers for someone.

The first time I asked for prayers for a very sick friend was several years ago. My friend, Steve S., had esophageal cancer and a huge love for his life, family and business. He clearly was not ready to die. Steve was told he had a 30% chance of survival. I had a small list of 12 contacts in my e-mails that I felt comfortable asking for prayers. I sent out a mass request for his healing.

Over the years I have put many clients on prayer lists for health, healing, overeating and various serious situations. As you can guess, Steve made a full recovery. He later e-mailed me that my request was one of the kindest things anyone had done throughout his illness. Last year I had another friend who was very ill and sent out a personal requests for prayers. This time I had more than 80 personal contacts that I was comfortable asking for kind thoughts, prayers and support for healing.

Simple Fat Burn Concept: The power of prayer can never be underestimated.

PART VII:
What's Next

21. Writing Your New Story

Now that you have more information about your motivation, your nutrition, your exercise and your consciousness, ask your-self has your story changed? Have you changed the way you think and feel about food, exercise and the actions that you take to create a better you?

Now, let's try the "I Am" exercise again and see how it compares to the one that you originally created. You may find that everything is similar, or you may find that you have created great change in your thoughts. If so, you can replace your original with this new, better definition of you.

WHAT TO DO
1. Spend a few minutes in a quiet room. Sit quietly and reflect on where you are right now in your life.
2. Fill in the blanks below with the words that best describe where you are right now.

SIMPLE FAT BURN

I am _____

I see _____

I feel _____

I am _____

I have _____

I understand _____

I try _____

I am _____

I say _____

I do _____

I do not _____

I am _____

3. Review what you just wrote and place a star beside the things that you are happy and satisfied with.
4. Put your story in a place where you can see it.

22. Making It Work For You

Simple Fat Burn is truly meant to enhance the quality of your life! It will change the way you operate mentally, physically, emotionally, and socially with your personal nutrition and fitness program. It works on men, women and children. It asks that you take your nutrition and fitness seriously and prioritize your health. It is straightforward, honest and truly based on the science of nutrition and has been proven by hundreds of clients over a period of 17 years.

What about the foods we love that are not on the low glycemic plan? Simple Fat Burn is not about deprivation. Yes, you are going to enjoy an occasional homemade piece of cake, a slice of fresh baked bread, a piece of quality chocolate or a glass of wine. Always go for quality over quantity. Get the meals and the baseline correct. Follow the plan and enjoy a small amount of the foods that make life enjoyable and fun!

Practice moderation and be conscious of your thoughts, feeling and behavior with confidence. You will learn to know how much you can consume AND feel good while continuing to get your simple fat burn results. It is my greatest hope that those who have struggled with diets, who have lost and gained body fat, will end any and all struggle by embracing these concepts.

There is an answer and a solution to every problem. The solution is not in processed foods, 100-calorie snack packs, or counting calories while ignoring content. It is <u>content, not calories</u> that makes all the difference in your success. The answer lies in eating natural foods that do not spike insulin, daily exercise as well as conscious, mindful behavior that promotes a higher level of health and fitness. Trust the process, and believe in your success.

Biography

Cathryn E. Marshall has been passionate about fitness and personal training for almost two decades, having trained hundreds of individuals to become fit and lean. She herself has competed three times in NPC figure competitions. Cathryn has spent several years managing personal training programs and mentoring many personal trainers. She received her BA in Sociology from SUNY at Fredonia, and her MSW from the SUNY at Buffalo. Her true talents are being a catalyst for positive change and in designing personalized programs. Cathryn is an avid professional networker and has served on the board of the American Business Women's Association. She currently lives in Duluth, GA with her son, Cameron.